Dangerous Diseases

Whooping Cough

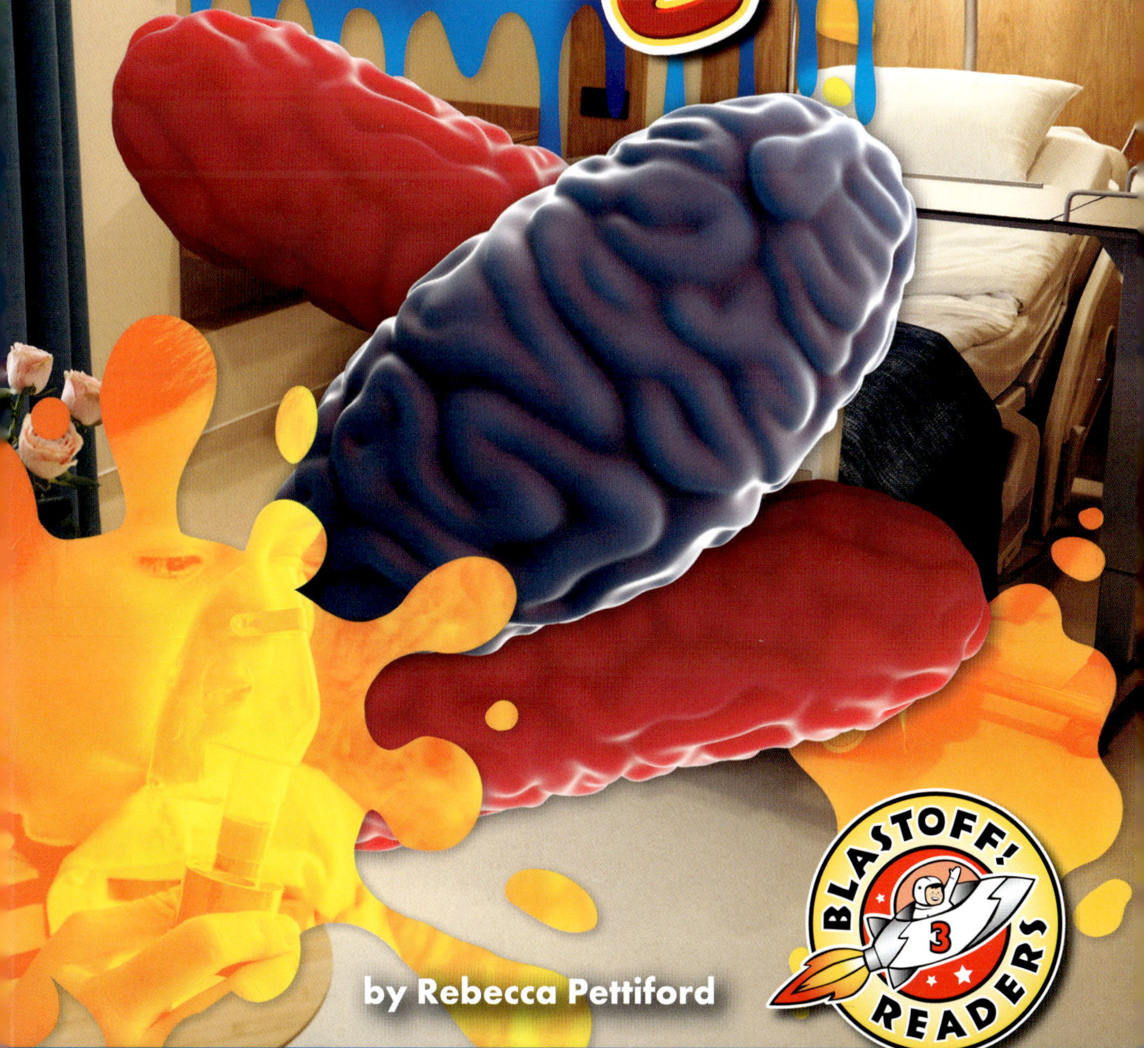

by Rebecca Pettiford

BLASTOFF! READERS, AN IMPRINT OF BELLWETHER MEDIA BY FLUTTERBEE

Blastoff! Readers are carefully developed by literacy experts to build reading stamina and move students toward fluency by combining standards-based content with developmentally appropriate text.

Level 1 provides the most support through repetition of high-frequency words, light text, predictable sentence patterns, and strong visual support.

Level 2 offers early readers a bit more challenge through varied sentences, increased text load, and text-supportive special features.

Level 3 advances early-fluent readers toward fluency through increased text load, less reliance on photos, advancing concepts, longer sentences, and more complex special features.

★ **Blastoff! Universe**

Reading Level

Blastoff! Beginners — Grade K → Blastoff! Readers — Grades 1–3 → Blastoff! Discovery — Grade 4

This edition first published in 2027 by Bellwether Media, Inc.

For information regarding permission, write to Bellwether Media, Inc., Attention: Permissions Department, 3500 American Blvd W, Suite 150, Bloomington, MN 55431.

Library of Congress Cataloging-in-Publication Data is available at www.loc.gov or upon request from the publisher.

ISBN: 9798898800680 (hardcover)
ISBN: 9798898801922 (ebook)

Editor: Suzane Nguyen   Designer: Brittany McIntosh

Printed in the United States of America, North Mankato, MN.

Table of Contents

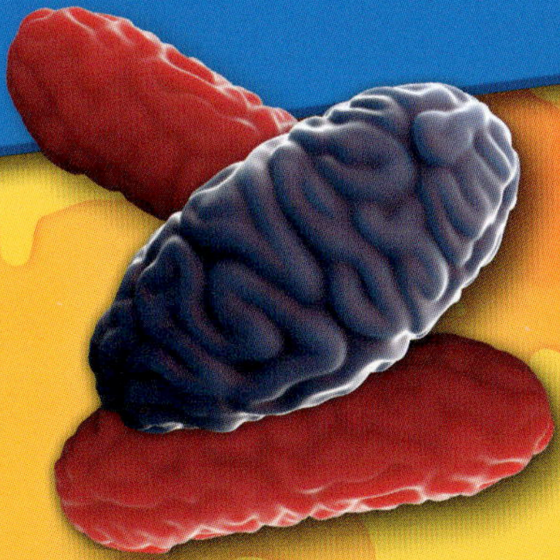

What Is Whooping Cough?

Whooping cough is a childhood illness. It affects the breathing system. It is caused by a **bacteria**.

Whooping cough is also called pertussis. Early signs are a low **fever**, cough, and runny nose.

After one or two weeks, people get worse. There is a lot of **mucus** in the lungs. It makes people cough a lot.

In a Name

Whooping cough gets its name from the whoop sound people made when trying to breathe in after coughing.

Coughs can last weeks or months. The coughs make people very tired.

History of Whooping Cough

getting a vaccine

In 1906, scientists found what caused whooping cough. The first effective **vaccine** for the illness was made in the 1930s.

In 1948, the whooping cough vaccine was improved. It was combined with two other vaccines.

Before the vaccine, whooping cough was one of leading causes of childhood illness in the United States. There were about 200,000 cases a year.

By the mid-1970s, there were fewer than 3,000 cases a year.

How Does Whooping Cough Spread?

Whooping cough spreads when an **infected** person sneezes or coughs. Droplets from the sneeze or cough move through the air.

People breathe in the droplets. They touch things that have droplets. They get sick.

How Whooping Cough Spreads

By Air

1 Someone coughs or sneezes.

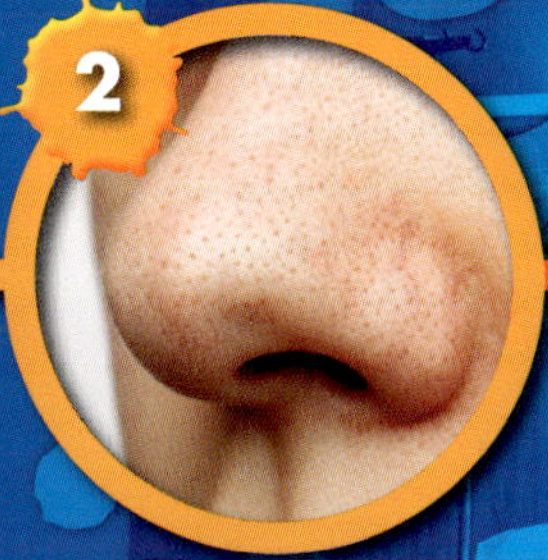

2 Droplets in the air enter a person's mouth or nose.

3 Person gets whooping cough.

By Touch

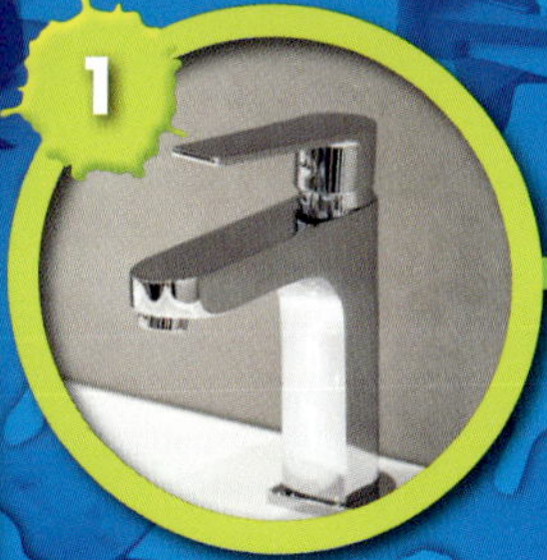

1 Bacteria on object.

2 Person touches object.

3 Person gets whooping cough.

Whooping cough has three stages. The first stage lasts one to two weeks. Coughing fits start in stage two.

People get better in stage three. It can take 10 weeks for people to get better.

Treatment and Prevention

People should treat the illness fast.
People take **antibiotics**.

Smoke and dust can make coughs worse. A **humidifier** can loosen mucus and calm coughs. Drinking liquids such as water and soup helps too.

Many children get vaccines. A vaccine is the best way to avoid whooping cough. This shot is a weak form of the illness. It causes the body to make **antibodies**.

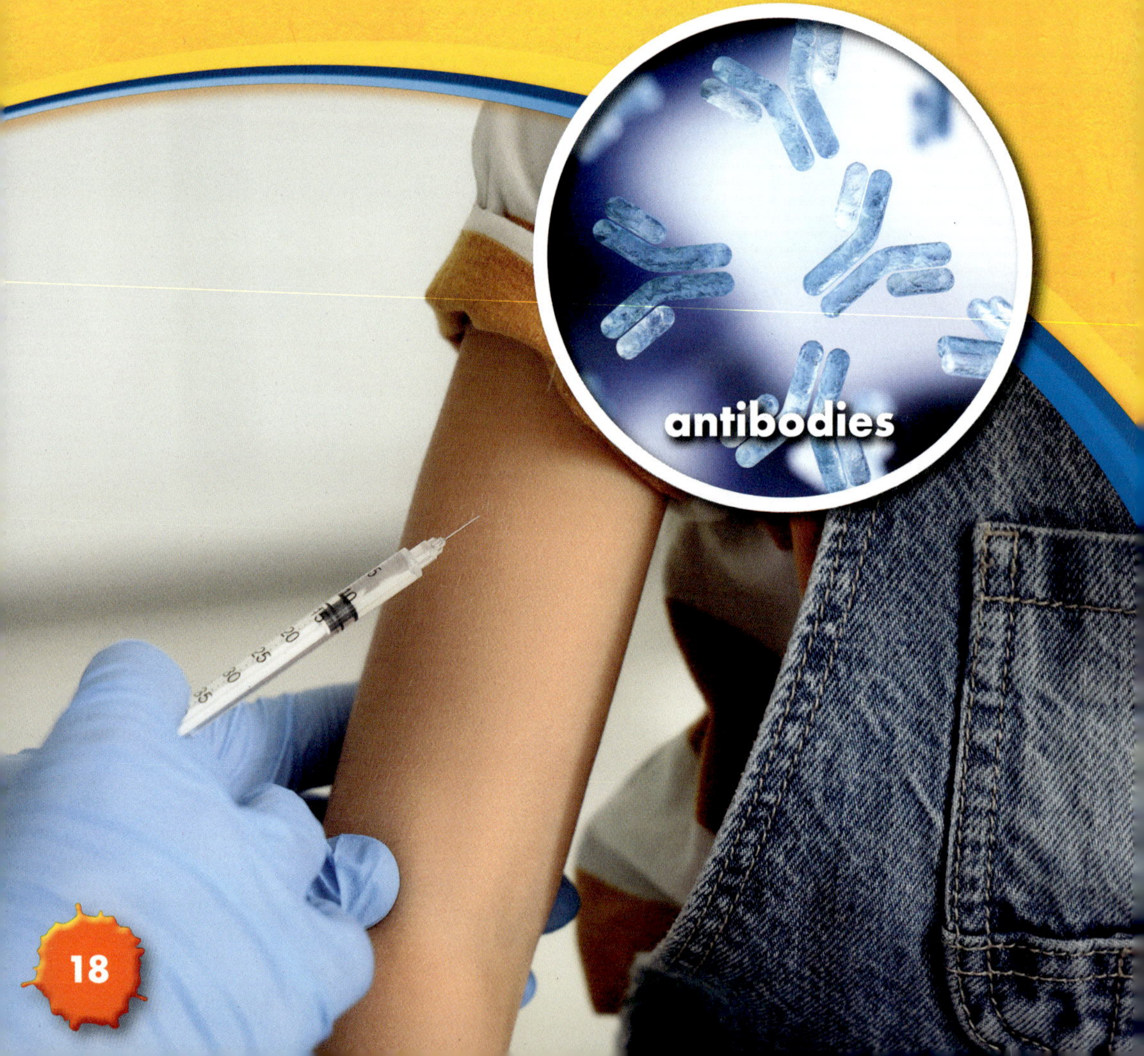

Healing Heroes

Name

Doctor Pearl Kendrick
and Doctor Grace Eldering

Year Helped

1940s

How They Helped

They combined the whooping cough vaccine with two other vaccines.

Antibodies help keep people healthy. These people are less likely to get whooping cough.

Whooping cough is worse for young children. Today, there are more cases in the U.S. because some children are not vaccinated.

The best way to stay healthy is to have several rounds of the vaccine!

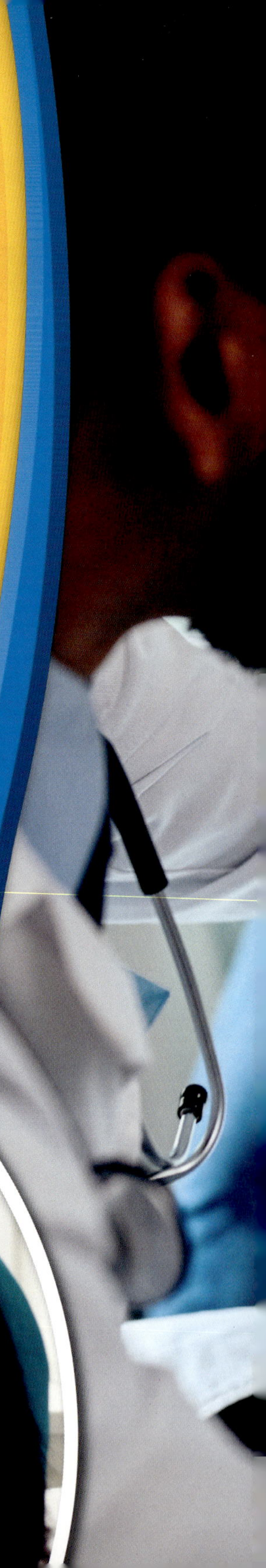

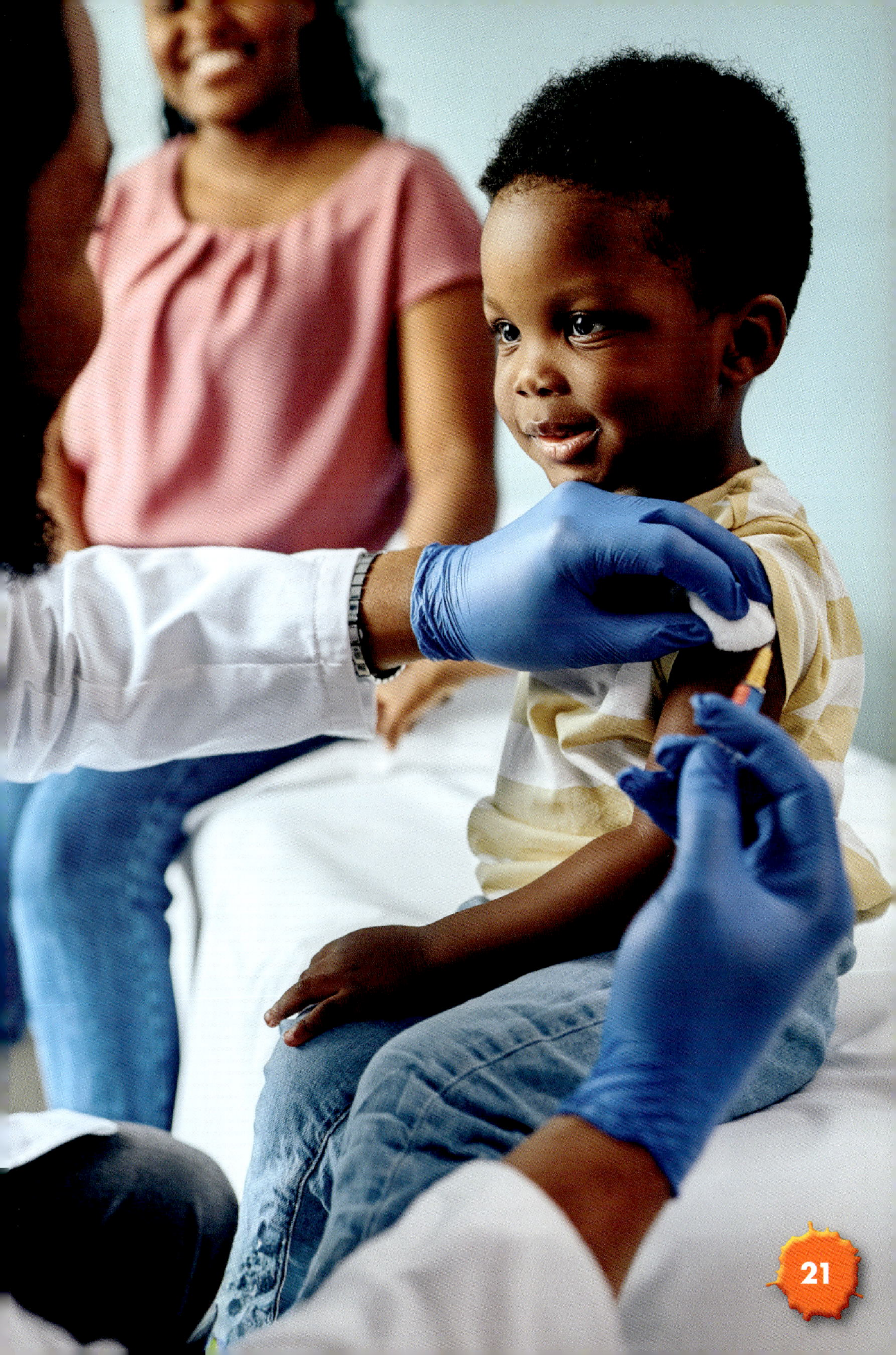

Glossary

antibiotics—medicines that treat infections caused by bacteria

antibodies—materials that the body makes to fight illnesses

bacteria—tiny life forms that can make a person sick

fever—a higher-than-normal body temperature

humidifier—a machine that adds water or steam to the air to make it less dry

infected—sick with a harmful illness

mucus—a thick liquid made in the nose, throat, and lungs

vaccine—a substance that is put into the body to help fight off illnesses; a person who has gotten the vaccine is vaccinated.

To Learn More

AT THE LIBRARY

Mould, Steve. *The Bacteria Book.* New York, N.Y.: DK Publishing, 2024.

Pettiford, Rebecca. *COVID-19.* Minneapolis, Minn.: Bellwether Media, 2027.

Troupe, Thomas Kingsley. *What Would Happen If You Never Got Vaccines?* Mankato, Minn.: Amicus Learning, 2024.

ON THE WEB

FACTSURFER

Factsurfer.com gives you a safe, fun way to find more information.

1. Go to www.factsurfer.com.
2. Enter "whooping cough" into the search box and click 🔍.
3. Select your book cover to see a list of related content.

Index

The images in this book are reproduced through the courtesy of: PRB ARTS, front cover (hero), p. 3; Prostock-studio, front cover (splatter top), p. 6; Helen Sushitskaya, front cover (splatter bottom); Svitlana Hulko, front cover (background); antoniodiaz, p. 4; Kateryna Kon, p. 4 (inset); PeopleImages, pp. 5, 11; Somkid Saowaros, p. 7; Studio Romantic, pp. 8-9, 20; Ola List, p. 10; 9nong, p. 12; joshimerbin, pp. 12-13; Pixel-Shot, pp. 13 (by air 1), 18; Marina Demeshko, p. 13 (by air 2); SofikoS, p. 13 (by air 3); Summer Paradive, p. 13 (by touch 1); Kostikova Natalia, p. 13 (by touch 2); panadda design, p. 13 (by touch 3); FAMILY STOCK, p. 14; suriyachan, p. 15; Odua Images, p. 16; Sharomka, p. 17; Svetlana Khutornaia, p. 17 (inset); ustas7777777, p. 18 (inset); Well/ BOT/ Alamy Stock Photo, p. 19 (top); Grand Rapids Public Library/ Wikipedia, p. 19 (bottom); Drazen Zigic, pp. 20-21.